PRETEND CART

Alicia Byrne Keane is a poet from Dublin, with work published in *The Moth*, *Banshee*, *The Stinging Fly*, *Boulevard*, *Stand*, *Acumen*, *Anthropocene*, and *The Colorado Review*, among other journals. Alicia's poems have been nominated for the Pushcart Prize, the Best New Poets Anthology and the Best of the Net Anthology. In May 2023, Alicia was selected for Ireland's National Mentoring Programme.

© 2023 Alicia Byrne Keane. All rights reserved; no part of this book may be reproduced by any means without the publisher's permission.

ISBN: 978-1-915760-52-4

The author has asserted their right to be identified as the author of this Work in accordance with the Copyright, Designs and Patents Act 1988

Cover designed by Aaron Kent

Edited by Kit Ingram

Typeset by Aaron Kent

Broken Sleep Books Ltd
Rhydwen
Talgarreg
Ceredigion
SA44 4HB

Broken Sleep Books Ltd
Fair View
St Georges Road
Cornwall
PL26 7YH

Pretend Cartoon Strength

Alicia Byrne Keane

Broken Sleep Books

Contents

Resolving	9
Or	11
surface audience	13
Strands	14
Shale	16
Filament	17
Wildflowers (I'm not sure)	19
Bull Island	20
Temenos	22
Draw a tree	24
Unspeak	26
McAllister's Garage	27
Sensor	29
String	30
Unpicked	31
Frond	32
Observatory	33
Dead orchid flowers, piano nobody has tuned [...]	34
Egg	36
Rime / Ripe	37

Leafblade	38
Sapindale	39
Nightshade	40
Apple, amber, amble	41
Shaky	43
Crabapples,	45
Close quarters	46
Sunset synonym	48
Tine	50
Preserver	51
I have started a meditation course called [...]	52
Hydrophone	53
Pedestal	55
Phoenix Park	56
Meadow	58
Algae	59
Sticky terms	60
Unbridging	61
Acknowledgments	65

Resolving

> What are you
> > thing like a sewing machine
> > thing like a writing desk
> > thing like an ironing board?

Where the forest steps back from itself
I remember you, here like a video game
portal, centre stage in the gold undergrowth.

The sun has concentrated in your flat weight
rust-bleached, and I am only now looking at you
properly, full of silent corners that invite rupture.

You exist in the blind edge I run past head canted,
angling into the showerhead warmth of song, your
shape resonates from my first walks around this

archive of dimmings, a quarter-century ago
you swam out of my boredom, a marker
in the woodland, those muddy traipses whose ends

I couldn't wait for. Back in the kitchen where
the dog skitters, fresh from the damp air. I think
of sometime in the middle, when I was, say sixteen,

the bright borders of fields as I sweated, wanting
to throw my navy jumper into the high-contrast plunge
of shade, bluish brush. I was elbowing out of the fine

limbed lines along which we observed ourselves
at three-quarter turns in the tiled murk, there were
hand sanitiser dispensers left over from an earlier

sickening, a panic last decade that wavered into
elision. I am sidelong through time as I look
at your amber shape, the slot and lever suggesting

haunted motion. Your equilibrium is inexplicable:
ghost-loom, gymnasium horse, surgical slab.
You look paused mid-resolution, there is a part of you

that arches wrongly. If I stare longer I will fix you
in dream-language, if I take a picture I can go home
to ask, *what does this do, this iron woodland table.*

Or

I

I don't know whether I had a good time, socially
in the black velvet warren where stairway scrolls
unfolded endless, where things were limned and the
glare formed bulbs or traces, dissolving to bible edge

gilt by a process I couldn't imagine. Everything was
miniature, and everyone watched with tiny faces. Once
I waited outside the bathroom here for a while, for a
date, or maybe not, but I always feel a fizz of useless

energy when standing beside glass cases, silent for
someone to finish reading the printed paragraph, or
aware of the division. A denuded version of my face
getting reflected, made into halves, or a thing like an

orange segment, partially removed and about to light
sour incandescence if you look at it for too long.
I would view cyan plates, stilled substances that look
lit from a vague place, a door telescoping. I would

fidget, if given the chance. Thirdness doesn't always
contribute in the way you think it will, the shining
outlet where our eyes fasten themselves and narrow
to a burnt point. The spindle and twist of a golden

ornament that someone has scratched chevrons into.
All I want is for some sort of protocol to appear and
tessellate its endings in my direction. Or I want the
directed shimmer to speak without recalling erosion.

II

(or I want the directed,   shimmer to speak without recalling erosion

or I want the directed shimmer to speak,   without recalling erosion

or I want the directed shimmer,   to speak,   without recalling erosion

or I want the directed,   shimmer,   to speak without recalling erosion

or I want the directed,   shimmer,   to speak, without recalling erosion)

surface audience

                        snow-blind bulge of water
                 surface helical or like a
                                   funhouse mirror

on the hudson bay a pod of seals surround our boat
in their hundreds   i am worried the whole time in a way
i can't describe   the presence of so many heads
turned
in our direction
coming to their   polite points   and earless too
                              or i guess
                                      they have
                                ears but
the thing about that wait is you cannot locate a word in
it   you cannot strain light through its more porous
parts   it is just a clutch of individuals knotting their fear
             and the sudden sharpness of promontories
in the distance
i won't remember anything else about that day   except the
interior of a restaurant cavernous and spaceship-like   there
is always such a feeling of accelerated doubt when you put
your first foot on to a moving vessel   i always
think i can
rehearse the motion   plan for it   or calculate how much
the waves would plunge at a greater speed   so those
first few
                                seconds are horrible

Strands

This has always been a wash of
                             ; there has always been a wash of
weeks where we shelter
fragments of the deleted

                     weight like a ball and socket
                     things welling water

the beach is lit with an interior gold
a meteorite scatter that loops through
the marram grass, tries its best   /

the lemon pebble dash of the
outdoor changing room looks enhanced
and overflowing, beacon of a   retina   answered

I think of waits and silences,
the long homes of razor shells
and how they look scraped,   a dirty adhesion   like
peeling

paint
remember the summer I spent
varnishing fences, dipping brushes into
the sour pour of a thing like   chemical honey
stilled

making something all the same
                     (and making a thing
                           look all the same way:
                           conform)

limned and oozing strength like a
closed wing, a covering of translucence

                                        was calming
                                        in the face of absence
                                        but I know I fantasise

because when I came back nothing was normal
the band broke up, and the relationship remained over

despite all its original ons and offs

and all I am doing currently is
looking at how rockpools hold sky
in the pictures

Shale

Today is like others, lengthened:
follow the headland to where it gusts into the sea

        and hope no parts of you break
        and hope no parts of your phone break

knowing the way home will be full
of gradated sunsets visible through cracks in gates

        (long and full of other peoples' gardens,
        their overheard space)

last weekend I tried to draw wasps
and this weekend I will try to draw conch shells and periwinkles

        I have not moved on from segmented things
        beings that involve both bulb and swirl

the sand, a conversation's rush:
mashed bottle-green, curving

        violet burst of a fragment palette-ridged
        storm cloud shrunk to a pebble, cooling

blue, a property that always seems held carefully,
resides at deepest inside, at settled floor

Filament

trajectories echo
on the flung glass;
new measures promised

the bathroom filled
with the speech of beads   (trailing ailing
cracking into corners   bailing sailing failing
    wailing jailing whaling
a hand is just   paling)
collected rectangles
when you draw it

sparks but not,
hold us paused
in the minute's hollow   (impaling)

white tile amplifies
some things and damps   (unavailing
others, all the baths   countervailing regaling)

i ever took here elongate
into an ocean when
placed end to end   (curtailing, prevailing)

(when timed, end to end)
i will become twisting
steam if i continue

stunned in the doorway
at the noise like sticks
purred along railings

hailing the stones
in their zigzag impact;
clean as pills, as mints

(flailing greyling.
quailing, scaling;
availing, derailing;
inhaling, emailing.)

Wildflowers (I'm not sure)

This crush scattered screams a bruise
through the dark of meadow, meets
thrown light in the hard space under
the chestnut branches. Their rush is
between stone kern and dry planet,
stuck in bunches so I think dreadful
catastrophe, hurt rubbish. (This wry
sun absence a grey drought scruff.)
They stay there somehow hardy and
stubbornly loving, faces turned in a
constellation towards drizzle gusts.
They speak in cloud underbellies, in
periwinkle circles under eyes, in the
tumbling blush of a fruit's ripe side,
in the kite-slivered language of new
things. They furl the sharp turn of a
tongue, and it spreads sea-depth, an
indigo fathom and what you might
find there. Like: the tide captured in
a bowl and funnelling sharp threats
of birdcall. We are painted-looking
things but not fake, also, we know the
stung pointillism of breakage, we've
practised it again and again, and its
flavour is sloe-bitter, slow-burning.

Bull Island

This afterlife is a gentle one:
all we do is look for dry places,
 for the concrete lip
that silences a raincoat's smatter.

We meet in sipped increments,
untouching and exhausted
from months of this.

Sometimes a ship sends breath
 from the bay's wide side,
five waves roving in a pod
knife dark fins through the seam.

We will know this disturbance,
know the push of containers
across water,

 the circuits
that have brought us to each other
and how they are frayed in places.

The lapping
stalks a windless stretch,
the moon turning over in sleep.

 Funny how airports
 weren't the problem in the end,
funny how I memorised your face
in the dead hours,
convinced a wash of drizzle
would breathe itself into my room:

          I'd become fixed
          in the sea god's gaze,
      curl silent as a catastrophe.

    But we were fine in the end,
only enclosed, only unable to
hold hands.

Temenos

           is the name of the surgery,
the street is a jewelled neatness
of bookshops,

I know the doctor's number
off by heart and I can't afford this
synaesthesia of fours and nines
showing up yellow ochre
or plum-bruised
in the clang
dread makes.

Ringing the doorbell
becomes a remembered tree-shadow:
we've entered the adjacency,
unwrapping a grove
from taut silence.

I know the doctor's number
off by heart, although I shouldn't,
the rules don't apply here
in the unresolved:

my fear something
I scramble to reach the edges of,
cloth in wind.
Assess the parameters
of what is hallowed;

pace the shell-pink outline of a diagnosis
that seems either terrible
or nothing at all,

depending
on the
shapes
of newly-spun
branches stilling the blue
above   you
as   you
   drive   home.

Draw a tree

                was the instruction,
            even though the wind
      tethered me to one bright corner
          of the sitting room,

it being my duty to
watch the sky's stop-motion flicker.
        Measuring the unpeeled parts,
    the quicksilver newness
they yawned,

I realised
both trees and leaves
are river-shaped,
one pulsation
mimicking another.

    I was never good
at shading, my crest of breath
would find itself in the gusts outside,
in the kitchen's blasting stir,
in how the lid of the bread bin
would threaten noise
then resettle.

I can't remember my tree at all,
was it archetypal, did it cloud
    itself emoji-like
        into a fine-leafed
sphere,
        did it twist across pages
or occupy a vacuum, taken

    from some soundless
Magritte background,

        a place empty of roars:
      the candle flames of poplars
          stilled towards sky?

Unspeak

For this one, there is   no   reframed sentence;
there is no contingency plan. Your departure
is an endpoint that has threatened to swallow
me with its silver tide for   as   long as   sips and
suns and sand. For as long as   flame-coloured
roses have existed, as long as rock   has pressed itself in layers
by the coast here, the marram grass   flocked   with stars.
Everything holding its tongue at the vowel's edge,
your departure is the unimagined, the one thing to avoid.
I have felt its arid shape in my sternum for so long.   I
have never looked at it, or let it laugh. I   have
never sat with it and accepted its echoes. I scan
the street: none of the   headlights   turning inquiry
to the silk tarmac are yours. Car-surface   a liquid
knife: I've never stopped   asking, asking   for your presence
to continue. I am still here asking as time and excuses
lengthen themselves into the evening like
cats. I will always be here after everything ends.
Purple-tipped grasses   loop a   softness   through
these fields; my outsides catch   glare in the weirdest way.
I imagine a graphic of your car dispersing into wind, undoing
its sea-crumpled wings. How   does a person   disappear?
The evening has an underneath. The evening   disappears
underneath people,   disappearance   is an   evening,
we disappear entire evenings because we are those
kinds of people; it's that simple. Evenings people
disappear. Evenings, people: disappear. No.

McAllister's Garage

Around here a wait is always violet-coloured,
mostly strung on necklaces and crumbling
to sugar between teeth. The flowerbeds
new, I think, speaking to headlamps
in their starred tartness. There's
a way light diffuses across
this mess of one-way
signs, the thick
network of
icing
on

the
tarmac,
that crumples
my 18th birthday
to a music-thick corner.
I knew the scorched orbs of
streetlights, I knew the waiting
space of the estuary, and little else,
and that's okay. I have come to realise
that was okay, I wasn't so disastrous, I was
only waiting for evening to come and delineate

> things. McAllister's Garage is somewhere I have never
> been inside, I have only seen the dim objects on
> display at a remove, I have only measured
> lateness by the sip of minutes at this
> traffic light, by the red and black
> loom of paintwork against
> an overcast morning.
> The bright nectar
> of rain has
> slipped
> to

gutters,
the dusk is
powder blue, the
flowers are miniature
clouds of frilled mauve and
I am hungry in a way that I wasn't
in those days, I make time for fortifying,
for certain gaudy questions. I know all this
could be easily a picture of a place hushed under
waves, easily a coral reef that thrums with biting lives.
But it isn't, and people are driving back from the Pavilions,

                                                cars filled with
                                                the dim
                                                rattle
                                                of
                                                              shopping
                                                          bags

Sensor

        The light turns on in the garden
by itself, and a feeling happens, clawing:

an arc of arm can break so easily into droplets
and I'm the one thing moving in this grey level,
        L-shaped and looking at itself.

I'm only imagining meteorites
but peach-flavoured,
scudding a balm through fog and throats.

        A shower door can turn skin to cloud,
so I'm also thinking of the laptop I broke
full of reading lists spiralled to inner-eye black.

There are always those places
where worry jumps and drains:

there seems so much
sharing involved in a swimming pool now,
and all I can predict is my submerged mouth.

        In water we can carry and be carried,
                pretend cartoon strength.

String

I will think,
in retrospect,
that I made
these small noises
of untuning chime
with the way sun
startled into the room,
so I joined the two
in my mind,
but that might not be
how it happened at all.
A knit calm grows
in little breaths here,
tangling and freeing.
Sparks will unspool
from all the instruments,
slowed in the minutes
pending rain.
They have said
there will be
two weeks
of joyous pour,
unswerving.
I sit losing the day
with an inner-cheek
silence, a feeling like
two orange segments
peeling askew.

Unpicked

I watch the open palms of this park every evening
searching for confluences, so how have I never
noticed the gate lodge, closed arc, silencing itself
in a far edge: concrete, white roses, a clean-swept
yard? Shutters muted green like this is a respite,
churches full of slit absence, the nearness of horses.
Back in the new place, there's too much laundry
to do in a single day, too many questions filtering:
our common ground a heavy dwelling-place, grove
or river bight. When I saw you this morning
I knew a sun had gone in somewhere, but I wasn't
sure why – we meet at either end of this flustered
kitchen practising the right words for doorways.
Later I am telling myself to breathe, undoing my
own tasks in the shed, feeling stone within a bite
of shoulder. There are too many inventive closures
inside this shipwreck of a shirt, that cloth coaster
demanding things in the voice of a shell's whorl,
calling to a struggle of sea. I leave the drifted
crumples for later, let spaces collapse inside
fabric so the landscape will be softened on my
return. If only that could happen for all of us.
I get sad when I think the meditation app is just
effective because it's somebody speaking to you
tenderly, some years ago and in another country.

Frond

Everything here seems to prevent
in the language of patio cracks,
and that's even before I mention
the spiders (eight legs and eight eyes
seeming just too much to believe.)
I like to think I resist interpretation,
but in the twigged scramble
of this house, you ask where
all the best words have gone
(tea-blushed, embroidered with
lilacs.) The other day I realised
the towel I was using (folded
into a mouth, lifted to bunch wet
from the tips of hair) had been frantic
in my hands just a life ago (flattening
on surfaces, swiping a bloom from
tiles.) Now in sleep, I become mulch,
learn to speak as a clearing does,
house small thoughts
that disperse when a torch is shone.
I turn my laptop from where
the night layers itself, dream us
an interruption that moves in jumps.

Observatory

I know already what will happen –
the air deadening into road, the
wiped shine of table between us.
A dusk, once: mud frozen to peaks
and tributaries. You can see bike
tracks & I'll retrace, overthink
this corrugation of tires until
the light goes leaden: again, a
rise and swerve halting ankles
with its abruptness. Remember
when we hiked to the place that
scoops light at its centre, a well
above ground – we ran out of
feints and lace by the foothills,
ended up threading ourselves to
the tower's furthest height. If the
conversation lulls this afternoon
I will fold the glowing fibre of a
wing into my mouth, pretend the
wan stilling leads to sustenance.

Dead orchid flowers, piano nobody has tuned in a good while

there is
folding, definitely:
paper nautilus looking
in
on itself, veined in a
silence
both backbone
and bedside:

    if there is laughter
it's brief and florid, held
at a heart.

On the surface
(bulk, boatlike)
the slumped
bloom could be tissue
or lace,

does not reflect the
hard coursing
of water.

    I had
thought someone pruned
the dragon-tipped
sails when
spent,
becoming
art in the paucity
of wind,

           but I think these
           fallings happen
           by themselves,
           leaving a bare
        juncture, lakeshore
lonely as barbs.

I pick two imploded
stars glow-jawed:

nothing here holds
poison, and still I chart
inner saturation,
magenta
swirled
in the
shape of flight.

Egg

I keep a list of coincidences in my phone
like I can cloud the glow of rarities, try
to make the threat leap out of an object
via its flattest side – reconnection a thing
tea-lit, a tiny eye in the smoke-dark bulb
of a keepsake, the startle of ceramic. Maybe
this is why people draw: fix the luminous
where it curls and shivers. For the time
being, I am just concerned with igneous
weights and the issue of their settling.
Earlier, rib-propped, the dune of the
couch, this very expectant apartment.
A cold dart of a thing underfoot, a whole
solidness waning. I thought: this will
be something very unpleasant. This will
be a stilled pour or blade. But it was only a
capo, birdlike: I often try to make them
snap sleek, but they are always crotchety
and disappointing. Stiff hand, I imagine
rain in your image, metal weights on
rooftops hammering everything smooth.

Rime / Ripe

At the top of the inhalation
there is swoop & confluence,
a peak forest-soft from above.

I fought with you
in my head & made it spindrift:
maybe somewhere

in the narrowing bend
of flu season there's a frozen river
underfoot. Maybe I am likeable

when a compound word:
today I found a late ambering
we couldn't classify,

downloaded that app
that's like Shazam for plants,
found the entry for

'orange banana tomato.' *Now,
that is just three existing fruits,*
I thought. *That is just inadmissible.*

New terms refused, we let skin
become patina-glittered in a future,
find itself an evergreen mouth.

Leafblade

You have seen all my meals
today, how they solidify into
a healed landscape,
their stages of construction
until the nervous toothmarking.
Our eyes emanate stilled murk,
old plant-water: I hide the last leaf
of the orchid when it settles
yellowing on top of the wardrobe.
Its plane looks like a toy,
big and rubbery,
cartoonish in death. I want
more light than the lamps
offer, I chase shoals of it
around the room until we coalesce
into stems, stalks, stationery,
organised things funnelling life
elsewhere. I wait for the bulbs
to warm, blinking –
I think this can't get
any worse and then remember,
I know how it can, I have a few
ideas. The homeware shop
sold so many careful little things.

Sapindale

I slice an interruption in the side of this room:
I have forgotten to turn off the main light,
calm the island of its wire-ridged skin. Now
it meets sun here at the meekest part of the
ceiling, where two peach-slivered saturations
coil. There is only one letter between water
and waver, everything lit from the wrong place.
If you saw this nervous palm from a distance,
shucked from the rooms around it, unstacking
would sway you. Into a terrible bluntness, a
swoon - it could be any time of year right now.
The orange you left on my bedside table is
missing a river of rind. I think my way into
several underpinnings, the fibrous paper of
midday & the place where veins cling. The
ripped parts look like seafoam and I always
forget stage-fainting is all too easy, knees
hinged to speak recline as mermaids on rocks.

Nightshade

When I cut open the pepper
there is a silk staircase,
a healthy windpipe.
I no longer feel so incisive
now the fibrous dialogue of seeds
has replaced me.
I am happy, immaculate-celled.

There is a boiler closet near my bed
and now and then it flares with noise.
When someone uses the bathroom sink
a raincloud deflates near my left shoulder:
we siphon warmth from an argument
painted in small, unobtrusive colours.

Thinking as a bud feels different,
clearer and hungrier
with my waterway neurons.
I pick up a scrap of paper
drifted on the windowsill,
turn it over to see
the smallest picture possible,
a raspberry pillowed in leaves.
I realise this is the tab from a jam jar,
some pretty part
for sealing freshness in.
I can write all this, somehow.
My fingertips are still normal-sized.

Apple, amber, amble

Nobody in this TV show
reminds me of anyone,
and I am glad as trees.

I winnow November's shape
into a clean sentence,
hold stooped cores too long.

This is how
you tooth a deadening
to your own texture:
a spit-tangle bled clear,
its dishwater chill on fingertips.

I keep waiting
for a honeyed thing –
maybe it's me, solidifying
at the kitchen table
(so full of winged weights;
all these treasures mid-flight.)

Let's walk in the meantime,
sever the dialogue side-slip,
forget 2004.

Chandeliers are stilled
in dragonfly repetitions
across the road.

Here, glass makes the silence
lake-deep & inverted.

We can see both
plum-shadow and amber;
a hush stalled behind teeth,
the empty patience
of taps.

Shaky

The forest spun
& interlocking
turns headlights
to gem scatter
on the windshield?
This time-lapse dim
& reawaken
of the tree canopy,
the big flat feelings
that compose
this road? How
it lies unspooled
into the village?
The perfect sentence
from my dream
was gauze-woven
from paths and teeth?
One car waiting
at the crossroads
pencil lead or pearl,
way too clear
in the photograph,
distance flattens
itself & I am
thinking how
I spent a morning
in this waiting room
when I lived at home
during college,
I can't remember
the complaint?
The tentative sunset

décor? The place
trying hard
to be a nook
& not this seep
of rescheduling?
This cotton bobble
fastened to skin?
Adhesive scrape
where the needle
dipped? A full stop
like the blood made?
The smallest eventide
in the world? The
smallest event, even?

Crabapples,

all of you look tired, looks tired:
sore thumbtacks fermenting,
candied and toothlike

at the glowed place
where colours meet,
the startle around a sting.

I was never good
at finding the boundary
of mosquito bite and skin,

& some constellation corners
drift glacé cheer into tarmac.
Why do they look so unnatural,

lollipop-sticked and sticking?
Nothing like the sideways
slip of their name.

Somewhere
insides congregate,
become star-withered.

Close quarters

It's taken me so long to notice
this singe or seam accenting
leaf-blade

        cherry-dark & threaded,
a whole Wednesday reiterating
bloom as a toppled mass.

I try to draw the succulent
& find only twists or noodlings,
can't chart the swell

        of a pillowed growth
excluding the room. I bead water
into its tilt, do this over the sink,

aim for an unseen stoutness
anchoring the slant.
I can't see where the structure

leaves the earth,
I am posed several questions
on inhabiting, the wounded pour

of sap through a dream.
For now there are junctures
and a kind of fleshiness,

        a kindred enamel
in the flowerpot's tint, plum fog
or blueberry dust.

                I give up on the axis,
                     sing small songs
to wherever the heaviness cascades.

Ceramic an adjacent hush
in the end, no matter how wide
its blueness:

all the hours of this room
will move through me,
lightening.

Sunset synonym

The room absorbing a solstice:
I dream of unknown swathes,
moss or breath, the filtering
dimmed by leaves.

The room full of boxes in the dark:
a path becomes cobweb, migraine
swollen with dirty light. I spend
this introduction furrowed.

The room, a moment reaching warmth:
we extend infinitely. Starts, starlings
flit granular ahead, our oversaturation
sharp as beaks.

The room, yet more fizzled things
settling like skin into a truce,
a shallow hum of cells. I think
of the rift as glossy, new.

The room, all I want:
a whorl of rest linen scented.
I measure nightfall by the boiler's rush –
our crux is woven, a good place to curl.

The room a blistered rise:
kettle noise fixing us in a tightness.
I can't go about my business
in the morning's held gaze.

The room records our stances
where luminescence tilts:
here at the sink like clock hands.
Here at the sinking, cloistered.

Tine

Our November is so mild
when opened at one end
like this, night full of leaves.

I brush my hair
in the lee of the floodlit garden,
think, for now, in dissipation:

fog turning to a scrabble
on the mirror,
as we speak or don't,

as I claw
the honey-bright
insides of rooms.

A hand holds ovalled wood.
Waxy edges bounce outside
& I greet a shiver.

Plastic teeth separate
me into little roads;
the garden's outer bound
a hush galactic with lavender.

Preserver

Last night, a bareness hung with raindrops
appeared in the crept frame of my bedroom:

I understood this is where ghosts grow from
bulbed and oyster-rough. Even now

I can detect a certain quietness of the lung
as I wait for the vine to stop tapping my window.

'It's my fault, getting stuck with the ground floor,'
I'd said into the silence, 'the place close to all roots,

even those of the air.' This is a paraphrase –
I do not talk so metrically when terrified.

This Halloween, we bought the kind of gourd
that has a bobbling rind, lava-bright & seeming

to disappear in a twist of its own fizz.
I watch it now, from across the table.

It has resisted putrefaction in a way
that's really amazing – it's nearly December.

I have started a meditation course called the 'Regret Pack'

I look back through the photos
from when we performed certainty,
imbued powder fuzz with corners
to court heaviness, make face to facet.

It's a headlamp gaze, my brows
have swallowed sky a few years too late:
in 2012 everything had a galaxy on it,
nebulae snug over skin. How odd, really,

the starkest reaches of us. I count
the aqueous glitter-stings, furrowing –
maybe I long to reflect. Still, I don't like it
when 2016 gets too close to my eyes:

that fondness for ice-crunch, particles
settling themselves on a gelled night.
Slick tarmac-glint ridge, stern corralling
of brushes: it was punctuation, I guess,

it was better than nothing. Matte
& gloomy, I can't quite remember
how make-up gets sweated off. What
was I going for? Who let me out like that?

Hydrophone

After Katie Paterson's *"Vatnajokull (the sound of)"*

Now and then at night
a bedspring resettles
even though I am lying still:

the line has been installed
aiding your descent
to a fissured place,

the phone number works.
You pay international charges,
zap through spindrift,

undercurrent, dark.
A pint of water seems so solid
behind a sternum, your dream

of transfusion lingering
as an imperative: replace fever
bit by bit with units of life

from the fjord's thrum.
A few months ago
there was a shortage

of thermometers here,
a city unable to gauge
the heat under its own tongue.

In Iceland, we visited
the moss-blanketed ravine
where plates connected,

cupped our quiet in palms.
The conversation, then as now,
must be one-on-one,

the ice uninterrupted.
We haven't met en masse
in so long, I have renounced

my vying, I am running out
of things to say on walks.
Imagine the press of water

to a receiver, the hush
and creak, the hoax video
of a mermaid's hand struck

mollusk-flat to the porthole.
Greeting or intimidating.
We watch the sky in the mornings.

Pedestal
After the Nokia game 'Bounce'

I hate all the hummed lapses in this house,
hands bunching my hoodie's front pocket
as I wait for things to cook. Our interstice,
a sipped thing patterned in fake brick and
the wilds of a young sleep: window-crack,
a coastline's cruel yaw.   (zigzag, plunge)
At this age I
am most likely tessellating food categories:
the solid yoghurt on cereal bars always
seeming paused mid-drizzle. I know world
slips happen in the grit of shore-glint mainly,
mild and glitching;

                    I would love to see all
this once more, chipped obstacle course,
gentle falls, pixels toothing a sphere. Burst:
the bodies of water would make me lonely,
predictably, they were so unexplained.
But I always found
this warren becoming,
whenever I failed to change. (In all,
I'm sure the stuff is just white chocolate,
advertised in boxes that spill cornucopias
of apricots, hazelnuts, grains.)
Dragged weight
stalling at a ramp, before overreach
and soar, the mid-air linger. I'd always
get stuck in some vaultlike drop, become so
aware of the silence, impactless as dreams.
Unassuming as swimming-pool tile. There
was such convoluted warmth, and such sky.

Phoenix Park

Unlit space mimics
the tread of water –
ground & sky a polished spill,
our lack of bearings soft-eyed.
I feel nausea at the reach
of broken boughs,
sheer verges;
the city an amber wash
through the bedraggling.
That bicycle light turns my heart
sideways with a violin's wrench,
your arm a comet trail.
I never understand
how dark can equal delay,
a shutter speed ragged.
I refuse to look.
You are indicating a deer.
I understand, can't describe
the aversion: torchlit,
elbowy things. I would say
it is a reluctance
to seed the haunting:
you know, these blurs
have a subcutaneous way,
a shape uneasily removed.
I noticed it earlier,
the succulent's calm wither,
something moth-mouthed
about those few leaves
at the heart,
just rotten scrapes.

That, or a horse-wound
flicked on taut skin.
Caught wind: there is always
some new development.
If this all ends, really ends
in hooves drumming,
in a light-surge through
our frayed interconnection
I will try and find someone
to be kind to.
Even if we are tattered:
their presence a clutch
of unknown fingertips
dotting an ellipsis
through glitches, glass,
we will speak
across the lurid ink
of water damage,
creating little waits
for each other.

Meadow

I'd always just felt like eyes looking out,
I guess, I always felt like membranes.
The folded heft of your own nose
eye-caught and peach lit, mothwing
trailing in the torch beam: I am never
ready when someone walks into the
room, I am squeezing all the satsumas
to see which ones hide veined collapse.
The next time I prise segments from
knotted light with a thumbnail I want
to feel cleansed of endearments. No
rind to collect in a cupped hand, I've
always hated any food you have to
carry skinned memories of, allowing
your path through the house to go
parchment thin and bin-slumped.
I take so long to get used to unfamiliar
laundry smells: airy twists wrung to
a tooth's transparency. Maybe this
phantom - billowing - should bring to
mind a cadmium-bowled wonder, a
host of little appendages. What does
the average daffodil smell like? I may
forget, I may have never known, we'll
permit me that. Anyway, scrabbling in
the washing machine's ridged stomach
all I touch is sugar, filling me up to the
back teeth. A Thursday missing its zest.

Algae

In my dream where the wrack swathed us
we had just left somewhere pebble-dashed
& brassy with heat inside: spark-flit hearth
full of tiny breakages. I remember a splinter
catching in wool, bare floorboards, clutches
of beer bottles in the door's shadow. Last
night I held the unthinkable, thought my
way through all the disasters I could. When
embers make a shower, sometimes a word
retains itself within a closed eyelid: here.
Hush, flora, scum. I, soot, granite, heave.
Acceptance a footprint filling slowly with
silt; me, loving wholly even as fronds slip
between us & an immensity opens in my
left ear, the one that always pops. It's been
sand-whorled until now, this winter, it's
been real (hair in salted twists blood-sharp),
& the next sliver of strand you visit will be
gifted an autumn, love russet & abounding.

Sticky terms

each other's one exception,
each other's one luxury;
the words already seem old-fashioned,
we said 'outbreak' then like babies learning
little bargains: I blot wine from the glass-base
with one knee of my jeans;
I kiss the tin of rose-flavoured Vaseline directly,
there is something 1940s about this gesture
(reject the small riverbend of finger tracing lip)
friends say 'I wouldn't panic just yet'
& I wonder where the threshold is,
air pixelated with a bloodying orchid-faint.
It's like I work to build up all this calm
& it gets knocked askew so easily (like a hat)
I look at pictures in warm rooms from 2017
& am jealous of myself
& am embarrassed for myself
(at the start I said 'social distancing'
when I meant lockdown/stay-at-home order/
working remotely & they're different things,
I'd say like 'I'm away social-distancing in my house')
I look at the solstice kept at bay by floodlights
& how the branches hold the sky's rime-silver edge
in a fuzz of becoming,
& am jealous of the trees
& am embarrassed for the trees

Unbridging

i.

All week I've been counting
the adhesive coat hooks
in this house. Ghostly,
the way they leave you
with questions,

yellowing plastic & always
placed somewhere inexplicable.
Inches above the ground
or solitary in doorways,
any air they spear

might twist, scared
into the frost-slip
of a wait. I do the same,
refresh the news.
Rain slicks patio furniture.

ii.

I let cold layer
through the crooked space
of the sitting room, fling
the windows open, make
an angled carapace of us.

As a kid I'd imagine
the raindrops having races
& at least that is something
to narrate, the tributaries
on fogged glass,

the little map cut there.
I make videos out the window,
keep the storm clasped
so long it's like boredom
& bones, whispering damp.

Acknowledgments

I extend heartfelt thanks to the journals and sites that first published some of the poems in this collection. These dedicated networks offered much hope to me and others during the pandemic's uncertain early phases. 'Resolving' was published in *Wild Roof Journal*, 'Or' was published in *Bayou*, 'surface audience' was published in *Oyster River Pages* and was nominated for a Pushcart Prize and a Best of the Net Prize. 'Strands' was published in *Strukturriss*, 'Wildflowers (I'm not sure)' was published in *The Colorado Review*, and 'Bull Island' was published in *The Journal*. 'Temenos' won second place in the Oregon Poetry Association's Fall 2020 Contest. 'McAllister's Garage' was published in *Invisible City*, and 'Observatory' and 'Crabapples,' were published in *Dodging The Rain*. 'Sensor' and 'Rime / Ripe' were published in *Banshee*. 'Egg', 'Sapindale', 'Sunset Synonym', and 'Algae' were published in *The Stinging Fly*, where I was featured poet for the Winter 2021 issue. 'Nightshade' was published in *SurVision*, 'Close quarters' was published in *Empty House Press*, and 'Sticky terms' was published in *The Interpreter's House*. I am immensely thankful to writers Alvy Carragher, Sydney Weinberg and Sharon Black for their wonderful insight into and feedback on my work. I am grateful to have received Agility Award funding from the Arts Council of Ireland in order to complete this collection.

LAY OUT YOUR UNREST

Milton Keynes UK
Ingram Content Group UK Ltd.
UKHW042311010224
437116UK00005B/229